27 Online Side Hustles

Paul Getter

Renown Publishing
www.renownpublishing.com

27 Online Side Hustles / Paul Getter
ISBN-13: 978-1-952602-02-3

CONTENTS

Opportunities for Every Skill Set

So you've got a full-time job, or you're a full-time student, but you want to make some extra money on the side. An online side hustle is like a trusty sidekick that helps the superhero in the story (you) to defeat the evil super villain. In your personal story that villain might be bills; credit card or student loan debts; a job that you hate and want to eventually fire, and replace with a full-fledged online business; or just the fact that you don't have enough vacation money saved to visit Disney World's Star Wars Galaxy's Edge or send your brilliant, nerdy kid to Space Camp.

But just like the sidekick in any comic book or superhero movie, your side hustle needs the help and attention of the main hero (you) to grow and succeed. And superheroes always have to make sacrifices along their journey to achieve the big victory at the end of the story, the one that leaves the world a better place for truth, justice, and all that is super and heroic.

There are so many opportunities to make money with an online side hustle, it's really almost unbelievable. And what's more, the number of possibilities grows every year.

Today there are literal metric tons of people who just stumbled into making better money than their quite respectable, successful parents did at their age doing not only *jobs* that didn't exist ten or even five years ago. That would be amazing enough! But they're doing those jobs on *apps and platforms* that didn't exist five years ago. That's really something else.

The digital information part of the economy is blowing up so fast, and multiplying so furiously into so many innumerable, *previously inconceivable* new possibilities, that I would go so far as to say every single person on this planet who knows they're a hero deep in their heart, has an *obligation* to start an online side hustle, *even if they don't need the money*. So they can add some of their energy, their time, their attention, their emotion, and their mind to the momentum of the cosmic ecosystem that's miraculously unfolding on our planet right   now.
I think it's a duty they owe humanity. And I think they owe it to themselves, so they don't get left behind, because this beautiful thing is moving very fast. And it will pretty soon swallow up the entire rest of the economy, until there's no difference between digital and conventional business. We're getting very close to that point now and hurtling toward it faster every day.

The longer you wait to start participating in the digital economy, the greater the distance between you and that glowing future grows, and the more difficult it will be to catch up to where the rest of the world is at five years from now, even a year from now. Also the more crowded the field of competition will be on the most lucrative platforms. (Don't even get me started on what's going to happen when AI programs start doing their own side hustles about a decade from now. They'll do about a million side hustles at a time. Those things think terrifyingly fast, and they don't dream of electric sheep.

Because they don't need to sleep!)

So enough theory. The rest of this book is a very down-to-earth, cookbook recipe-style guide to each of the 27 online side hustles covered. You'll get some background information to help pick the one you like, and very specific, step-by-step walkthroughs for how to get started and begin pulling cash from your online labors as soon as possible. And tips for scaling and optimizing to grow that income stream into something substantial and sustainable. If you find something in this book that you love doing and you're good at it too, this might be the beginning of an endeavor that alters the entire trajectory of your life, and gives you freedom, power, and resources on a level you may have never thought possible.

CHAPTER ONE

ClickFunnels

Your ideal side hustle might be to sell a product or service online. You may already have something you want to sell online or have something in mind to create and sell. Maybe you make custom, hand cut silhouettes of people's kids for them to give as gifts to their spouses and parents. Maybe you want to sell an e-book filled with all of grandma's favorite recipes. Or maybe you want to sell a world-changing widget that you created in your garage.

There are literally infinity ideas that could generate you some extra coin. Coming up with a good idea isn't the hard part. In fact the majority of people probably have at least five good ideas that could do more than make them some extra income on the side. Most people have had several ideas that could make them a millionaire if they knew how to execute on them, and had the will power, energy, and tools to get the job done.

The idea, the product, the service, that's the easy part. But the reason why most people aren't millionaires or even successful side hustlers at something they really care about is they don't know how to sell. Sales is a very specialized skill, and almost no one has any training or experience selling whatsoever. Sales is something most people are terrified to do, or even feel negatively toward. Sales conjures up images of the cheesy, badgering, maybe dishonest used car salesman with slicked back hair and too much cologne who doesn't know when to take no for an answer. Most people don't want to be that guy, so they shrink from selling. But selling is the difference between a business that succeeds and one that fails. Every single time. Assuming the product or service is good, or even just good enough, it's the ability to sell, or lack thereof, that determines the successful or failed outcome of the enterprise. Here's the rub with selling online-- in some ways it's even more difficult than selling in person.

In person sales requires positive, open body language, good non-verbal communication, and lots of relaxed eye contact. To close deals, the salesperson has to immediately exude sharpness, enthusiasm, and expertise within seconds *before* the handshake. Then they have to be good at listening to their prospect's needs, presenting their product as a solution, answering objections, uncovering unspoken objections, and finally helping their customer to make a comfortable decision to buy the product or service they're selling.

When people buy things online, they go through a similar process, but all of it has to be done with text and multimedia on a page. Imagine the challenge the first people to sell online had trying to figure out how to establish trust without eye contact, enthusiasm without tone of voice, and warmth and friendliness without being able to smile at their web page's visitors.

But it can be done. The reason even more people fail at selling online than in person is they don't know all the things their web page visitor needs to know and feel in order to be comfortable making a purchase. And they don't know how to trigger the prospect once their buying temperature is hot enough to buy before talking themselves out of it or leaving their page to do something else and forgetting about it.

Here's the good news. Online selling has the one game changing advantage of digital media that in person selling doesn't. That is, it generates historical data about performance. The words in online selling copy, the page layout, the images, even the color of the checkout cart button can be (and sure have been!) A/B tested scientifically millions, utter billions of times across every product category and hyper-optimized into something that just works the best it possibly can to close any visitor who it's possible to close. Whether that's to get their email, or to earn their business.

And that's what ClickFunnels is. ClickFunnels is an online sales associate, who can outsell anyone out of the box. ClickFunnels helps you sell your products and services online. It's so good at what it does because it's the end result of all those previous tests ultra-refined into the perfect online selling method. Think of it like Netflix.

How does Netflix make such great television? This Internet startup with none of the experience of Hollywood and New York City television studios, that used to just mail people DVDs a few years ago now makes some of the most on-demand original shows and movies on the planet. How'd they get so good at making the kind of television and movies people can't resist binging in such a short time? They had something Hollywood never had. They had the digital data their users created every time they streamed. Netflix's platform logged every event when users streamed. Every episode they watched a second time. Every time they paused the stream. Every time they re-watched a scene. Then Netflix created data driven television. And it's even more addicting than broadcast television.

ClickFunnels helps online hustlers get more sign ups, and clients, and sales the same way. It's data driven sales. It's the end result of the accumulation of far more years' worth of online selling data and purchasing patterns than Netflix has on-demand streaming data and viewing patterns And it's put together to be super easy to use, a plug and play sale page that knows what to do for you, and automatically guides you to put your offer together into a pitch that gets results.

ClickFunnels has 26 battle-tested "funnel" (a sales page that takes a visitor through the steps they need to go through in order to convert) templates optimized and proven to deliver high conversion rates for Squeeze Pages (an offer of a free resource for a visitor's contact information), Sales Pages (to sell products or services), and OTO pages (urgent one time offers available for a limited time). Along with the templates and a very user-friendly, intuitive template editor, ClickFunnels offers website hosting, A/B testing, email auto-responding, integrated payment tools, lots of training materials, and customer support. Many of the other online side hustles in this book will offer some more in-depth, step-by-step guides, but ClickFunnels does all that for you so perfectly. It's so accessible, all you need to do is visit www.TheFunnelNerd.com and start the 14-day trial. Have some fun.

CHAPTER TWO

Steady

In 2017 an Atlanta-based startup envisioned a platform that's kind of like Uber, but for all kinds of jobs, not just ferrying people to and from the airport, or safely home from the bars. The company raised a few million dollars in seed funding from investors, including NBA superstar Shaquille O'Neal. But don't worry, the work on the platform is steadier than Shaq's free throw!

They launched "Steady" in 2018. It's like a much broader Uber platform, for any work that people and businesses need done on a one time, on-demand basis. It also connects side hustlers with temporary hourly jobs, and regular part-time work.

It's currently a Top 100 Apple App Store app in the Business category, so it's a thriving listing for side hustlers ready to take on some extra work. It's a great way to find something that can work flexibly with your main hustle and other obligations.

And signing up to use Steady comes with some extra benefits for freelancers and part time workers as well. Registered app users get discounts at partner retailers and pharmacies. And you also get a free year of services from Betterment, an online, automated financial advisory and asset management service that helps users put away money to save for retirement, or big purchases in the future like a dream vacation or house.

So here's how to use Steady. It's so easy. You can download the app from the Google Play and App Store. Or you can just go to their website at https://web.steadyapp.com/ and sign up there without downloading the app.

It's very seamless. You can search for certain kinds of jobs, or jobs nearby, and see some of the listings before you sign up, whether you're in the web version or the app. You don't even have to sign up to start using the app to view listings.

You will find a diverse range of jobs like: overnight dog sitting at your house or the dog owner's house through Rover; renting your car for cash through Getaround; renting out your pad through AirBNB; doing food delivery for Doordash; doing anything delivery through Postmates; working part-time stocking inventory at Burlington; writing part time about emerging technology for Inverse; or working a flex schedule as a health and wellness writer for Bustle.

That is just a tiny smattering of what's listed on Steady, but gives an idea of how varied the opportunities are. To get shown listings the platform's AI is pretty sure you'll be most interested in, just sign up to use Steady, and it will give you a survey that takes about 5 minutes to fill out.

It'll ask about your priorities such as getting hired quickly, getting paid quickly, or guaranteed hire. It'll ask if you prefer working from home, working in someone else's home, working in a business location, or working outside. And it'll ask about your work experience.

One of the stand out features of Steady, is once you sign up and begin taking jobs, it tracks your income streams and shows you the data in a way that helps you draw insights to optimize your work schedule and maximize your income through the platform.

CHAPTER THREE

Website Design

Here's a tip worth a million dollars to anyone who takes it and runs with it: Your city or town is full to the brim with small business professionals who make a huge amount of money and spend tons of cash to maintain their business every year, but have no idea how to design a website or run an ad campaign to grow their business.

Think dental practices, law offices (personal injury lawyers, tax attorneys, copyright lawyers, criminal defense attorneys, divorce lawyers, all the different kind of lawyers), doctors, chiropractors, certified public accountants (CPAs), home remodel contractors, lawn care companies, all kinds of businesses like this.

A lot of these small business professionals are the proverbial "millionaire next door." They have nice houses and cars, but they don't live beyond their means because they work hard for their money, and they are patient, frugal, prudent, temperamentally conservative people. These professionals are very conscientious, which is why they're successful doctors, and lawyers, and accountants. But they don't rank very high on creativity. They're more Blackberry than iPhone, more PC than Mac if you know what I mean.

To these people, if you can use a computer with any degree of competence, you are super impressive in that regard. If you can design a website, you're a wizard. Even if you have no idea how to write a computer program or code a website from scratch.

If all you do is get a GoDaddy account for web hosting, install a premium WordPress theme, read up on best practices for Search Engine Optimization (SEO) to help them rank their business higher in local search results, and make the website look nice-- you are an absolute nerd as far as they can tell.

These kinds of businesses are falling behind local competitors who are more web savvy or have hired their niece to do their website for them. They spend tragically vast amounts of money on lead generations services from old dinosaurs like the Yellow Pages that don't convert and get them the customers that kind of spend should get if they put the money into year-2020 relevant ad campaigns and had an up to date website that focuses visitors to a strong funnel page to fill their inbox with inquiries and make their phones ring.

So here's what you can do. Start going through local businesses that fit this kind of profile. Professional small businesses that likely have a fat budget but are spending it wrong. You know they're spending it wrong by checking out their website. If they don't even have one, Yahtzee. Send them an email, call them, and stop by in person asking if you can design their website for them. If they have one and it looks like it hasn't been updated since 1999, Yahtzee. For your first one, offer to do it for free or very cheap. Tell them you're just starting out a new website design business and you need to develop a portfolio of websites to prove yourself so you can start getting more clients and charging for your services. This is important. If you have no experience doing this so far and ask someone to pay you $1200 to design their website, you'll get a lot of rejection, get discouraged, and quit.

Then set up their web domain and website. Use one of the most popular web domain hosts with a good reputation and excellent customer support, so if you don't know how to do something, and have trouble figuring out how by Googling it, you can get support on the phone and they'll help you.

For me, GoDaddy was a life saver in this regard when I first started out designing websites for small businesses. How do I get the DNS settings right? I had no idea. But someone on the phone guided me through the process step by step. BlueHost, HostGator, InMotion, Hostinger, and Wix Website Builder are also great options. With Wix you have an easy to use website builder.

Don't feel like an imposter, and just be completely transparent about how you're building their website. They don't care that you're using Wix instead of writing the code from scratch. Almost no one designs a website that way anymore, and your customer has no aptitude or patience to even use Wix. Just because it's easy for you doesn't mean it's easy for them. They spent their whole lives from the time they were hitting the books in high school specializing in dermatology or something so they can pay other specialists to handle things like their websites.

The more your online side hustle grows and the more experience you get, the more sophisticated your methods will become, and the more you can charge. You can also update clients' websites with what you learn as you grow and continue to get recurring fees without having to put in the initial footwork of acquiring a new customer. One great way to find clients for web design is on Upwork-- which is the next hustle in this book.

CHAPTER FOUR

Upwork

If you want an online side hustle that's less of a "frontier," Wild West kind of situation like the website design hustle described above, wherein you're just going it alone, and creating the structure of your hustle out of the total chaos of pure possibility-- if you need something that has the structure built into it for you, then Upwork is a good way to go.

It's a massive platform that acts as a clearinghouse for freelance workers and people / businesses that need all kinds of different jobs done (ranging from one off projects for $25, to month-long projects, to part-time and full-time work). Unlike Steady, which has many in-person kind of jobs listed along with digital work from home jobs, Upwork is pretty much all digital remote work that can be done from anywhere in the world.

When I say "massive" I do mean massive. Upwork was formed out of a 2015 merger between eLance and oDesk, and it clears more than a billion dollars' worth of business between freelancers and clients every year. Every day, hundreds of jobs are posted for freelancers. If you're better suited to success within a structured platform versus striking out on your own, Upwork is ideal.

After signing up for an account and getting your identity and tax status and all that verified, you'll be able to search all the new jobs posted to Upwork every day and apply by sending a "Proposal" to the client outlining your qualifications and pitching yourself for the job. You can use Upwork's filters to break down the job search by category to find something you can do and are interested in.

The broad categories are: Accounting and Consulting, Administrative Support, Customer Service, Data Science and Analytics, Design and Creative, Engineering and Architecture, IT and Networking, Legal, Sales and Marketing, Translation, Web, Mobile and Software Development, and Writing. These are further divided into subcategories such as: Human Resources, Virtual Assistant, A/B Testing, Photography, Interior Design, Information Security, Contract Law, Search Engine Optimization, Medical Translation, Game Development, and Article & Blog Writing.

To send a proposal you have to pay a small fee (we're talking about pennies), and if you get a client, Upwork takes a commission out of what the client pays you. It's 20% on the first $500 you bill a client. If you keep working with a client, Upwork takes only a 10% fee out of earnings between $500 - $10,000 in lifetime billings, and after $10,000 the fee drops to 5%.

With your own web design business you get to keep all your earnings. No finder's fee gets taken out of your check for connecting you with clients. But that business does require a certain amount of faith that only people with the lunatic constitution of an inveterate entrepreneur have. There's more initial work you have to put in with less guarantee of results.

That is somewhat true of Upwork as well, but the initial time and work investment isn't as great, and the leads are delivered right to you on the platform instead of having to go hunting to find businesses to cold contact. They're also warm leads, people definitely ready to hire right now and actively looking for a freelancer to work on a job they need done.

To get the most out of this hustle, you'll want to put good effort into your Upwork profile. Google around for some of the latest advice on how to make an Upwork profile pop and use common sense. List any relevant qualifications. Think of it like creating a resume.

When just starting out, you'll have the best luck reaching for the low hanging fruit. Upwork has reputation scores and ratings for the freelancers and the clients. So you'll have to develop a track record by applying for the smallest, lower paying jobs first. Give it your all, do your very best, and make the client happy so you'll get a strong review and perfect freelancer rating. When you turn in your work, tell the client specifically, "If there's anything you're not completely satisfied with, please let me know and I'll get fixed the way you want right away." When they accept your work and thank you for your help, ask them explicitly, "You've been a great client. I'm going to give you a perfect rating and strong review. Is there any reason you can think of that you wouldn't be able to give me a perfect rating? If so, please let me know before you submit your review so I can make sure you're 100% satisfied with me and my work."

After you do a few lower paying, one off jobs and have some work history with a solid track record, you can start sending proposals for jobs that pay a little more, or are bigger projects, or both. With some history to show you're a good worker, you'll be more likely to land those gigs.

CHAPTER FIVE

Shopify

I'm going to start by telling you all the reasons not to start a Shopify for your Internet side hustle, but there are still opportunities left on this platform to make money from a decent side gig, and even to create a prosperous small business for the few who lean in far enough to grow their Shopify store to that point. There are a lot of Shopify gurus out there overhyping a lot of unrealistic expectations without giving quality guidance on how to approach the platform. So I don't want to at all look that part.

Instead of hyping some anecdote about a miserable office grunt who started their Shopify last month and is already making $450,000 a month, and quit their job this month to party on yachts with champagne for the rest of their lives, I'll tell you the truth: It is much harder to make money on Shopify today than it used to be. That's because the calculus has changed.

The costs of advertising keep making Shopify margins thinner. The era of instant six figure Shopify riches belongs to the yesteryear of super cheap Facebook ads. As Facebook ad prices go up, the game has gotten trickier. But that doesn't necessarily mean you can't succeed and even prosper on Shopify. It just requires some creativity, learning some new things, and problem solving. Doing what everyone else is doing will give you meager or tragic results. Doing something different-- if it's smart-- will net you profits.

The basic equation for Shopify stores is Profits = Sales Volume times (Sales Price less Cost of Fulfillment). And the more successful stores have high volume, high prices, and low costs. So solving the never ending volume problem for Shopify stores is a matter of driving more and more traffic at cost efficiency. If Facebook isn't cutting it for that purpose, you have to look at emerging platforms where there is lots of traffic, but where advertisers haven't crowded in yet and driven up ad prices.

Try looking at Reddit ads, Tik Tok ads, LinkedIn ads, and ads on other platforms that have thriving communities, but where advertisers haven't saturated the place yet. They have lower costs and can deliver highly qualified traffic. While others bang their heads against their desk because they can't eke out a living or even a miniscule profit on Shopify with their Facebook ad spend, you can do something different than the crowd by thinking about the problem a little and exploring the other options out there. The Internet is an ocean of human attention. Facebook, while certainly vast, is not the only place where you can get your share of that attention.

As for what to sell on your Shopify, drop shipping is a popular option. That's an entire online side hustle all its own in this book. So there's some overlap between that chapter and this one on Shopify. Read both together carefully if you plan on doing either for your side hustle. Drop shipping means taking orders, forwarding them to a fulfillment company that keeps the inventory in stock for you, and keeping the markup leftover after paying their wholesale fulfillment cost. Some of the biggest drop shipping companies include: Oberlo, Spocket, Modalyst, and AliExpress.

People sell all kinds of things on Shopify. Some of the hottest product categories the platform itself recommends in 2020 are shapewear, pet grooming products, athleisure apparel, smart watches, jewelry, and shoes. But a good approach to take would be finding a niche to build a brand around for long term success cultivating repeat business from a growing customer list. Instead of just trying to be Wal Mart or Amazon and offering everything (you can't beat them), find an underserved niche, something interesting to you personally, full of products you want for yourself, and make sure the products are something you can charge a high retail markup on.

CHAPTER SIX

Info Products

Creating your own, original information project is a great online side hustle for a number of reasons. The disadvantages are it is more of a risk-taking endeavor. There's not as much guarantee of success and immediate income as finding gigs to work on Steady or Upwork.

And it requires a lot more up front effort, and potentially some more up front cost depending on your approach, without an immediate payoff like finding some work in the digital gig economy. But creating digital info products does have a lot of advantages as well. That makes it a high-risk / high-reward proposition. Scarier dragon to fight, bigger pot of gold it's sitting on.

You've got to do what makes the most sense for you. If you need or want fast cash, this may not be the way to go. This will take time work testing and really not some "get rich quick" thing.

Info products themselves are more work up front to create. And there's more work up front to make your website for selling them, but once you've done the work and have your finished info product, you can sell it again and again at no additional marginal production cost to your time and energy. Can you say residual income?

Cha-ching. And if you've got a page that converts well when you send traffic to it, all you have to do is keep buying or generating more traffic, and you keep giving yourself a raise from your info product hustle.

So how do you go about deciding what info product to create? They say those who can do, and those who can't teach, which is a saying I just love since I teach people how to make money online. So I know how untrue it can be. The very best teachers are those that know what they're talking about. Those who have authority to teach whatever it is they're teaching.

If you don't believe that you have the expertise to teach people anything that they would be willing to pay to learn from you, that doesn't mean you can't create a successful info product. You'll just have to become an expert on whatever it is you intend to teach first.

The very best info products are those that teach someone how to solve a problem they have. So a paid webinar or e-book about the finer points of the Greek philosopher Epictetus probably won't sell very well. A good place to start is a problem that you already know how to solve because you've dealt with it yourself in your life or work. Or a problem that you have that you'd like to solve. You could lean into it, become an expert on it, and solve it, then share what you learned in an info product, and get paid to solve a problem that is important to you.

If no ideas are sparking yet, do some browsing through ClickBank.com (a good place to list your info product for affiliate marketers to sell to their email lists or on their blogs or video channels). The kind of problems that people will pay to learn how to solve usually fall under three broad categories: Health, Wealth, and Relationships.

For health there's weight loss, yoga, diet, exercise, weight training, and so many other possible info products. There's potentially huge money in good info products about these topics. Remember those ads a while back that were everywhere for "secrets to a flat tummy?" That guy made millions of dollars selling info products. He changed lives with a lot of really valuable health information. For wealth the possibilities are even more staggering.

Personal finance is one of the most profitable niches in the blogging and info product world. There's budgeting, frugality, paying off credit card debt, saving and investing, and believe it or not-- how to make money online. But there's also a million different business niches you could create an info product about: How to set up security cameras for small businesses like storage units or laundromats. How to flip used books online (that's a side hustle in this book). How to start and grow a successful lawn mowing business. You could actually double up on any other side hustle in this book if you decide to be an absolute monster and crush it, becoming one of the best at it, and then distill what you learn in the process down to an info product that teaches others how to succeed. The best info products are usually something that could be titled "How to…" and the best how to info products are actually how I did it info products.

The easiest way to make the product is in a word processor, and export the finished work to a PDF format and an ebook format. (Literally select File, then Export, and the file format to turn the document into in your word processor.) For your website to sell it, use Wix, Wordpress, Blogger, or ClickFunnels if you want all their added online sales support.

DURING TOUGH TIMES

EVERYTHING CAN- AND WILL CHANGE.

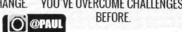

YOU'VE OVERCOME CHALLENGES BEFORE.

NOT GETTING WHAT YOU WANT CAN BE A BLESSING.

ALLOW YOURSELF TO HAVE SOME FUN.

THERE IS ALWAYS SOMETHING TO BE THANKFUL FOR.

BEING KIND TO YOURSELF IS THE BEST MEDICINE.

CHAPTER SEVEN

Blogging

The downside of blogging is you might get cold because there are so many drafts. Sorry I couldn't help myself. There are more opportunities to blog and make money on the side in 2020 than there have ever been since blogging first came into existence in the early 2000s. Short for "weblog" a blog is essentially just dated articles posted to a website in reverse chronological order. Today every business and publisher that's trying at all to engage its customers and audience, while staying on top of its search rankings has a blog and keeps it updated.

Starting your own blog could be potentially lucrative if you are an expert in a niche with an enthusiastic audience, or become one by blogging about it with dedication and consistency, but on average this approach is a failing strategy to make money blogging. And those bloggers that do make money this way usually take years to make anything worth speaking of.

The most sure way to hit the ground running and make money blogging is to write for someone else's blog. Upwork is a good source of leads for businesses and publishers looking to hire bloggers to write for their website. And it pays right away, per blog or per word. No sleepless nights for years scrapping together an audience in your spare time shamelessly shilling your latest blog to every other blogger in your niche.

Another great source of blogging jobs is the jobs board on ProBlogger.com. This has been updating every day for years with something like 2 - 5 new blogging jobs. Many of them are very high quality gigs that demand excellent writers and pay very well. Competition is stiff, so bring your A-game when sending your application and resume. Writing for free at first to build up some writing samples is not a bad idea. Just one month of doing this in your spare time can get you started with some work history to show potential new clients.

Other good sources for a never-ending stream of blogging job posts include the jobs boards at BloggingPro.com, FlexJobs.com, Indeed.com, SimplyHired.com, MediaBistro.com, Writers.work, FreelanceWritingGigs.com, WritersWeekly.com, AllFreelanceWriting.com, and JournalismJobs.com (search "remote" in the search bar for remote jobs to work from home). iWriter.com pays as much as $80 per 500 word article to its top writers.

This is a job you can do from home as a side hustle and slowly grow your experience and resume into a full time career if you want, or keep it as a side hustle in addition to your day job, and make extra money, or all your income to pay all your bills forever. There is an endless need for copywriting and blog writing to fill all the space online, and the capitalization to pay bloggers for it.

Some people who've tried it may say you can't make any money blogging. They are so wrong. They gave up too soon, or didn't have the aptitude for it (basic command over English grammar, spelling, mechanics, punctuation, and usage-- and the ability to write interesting blog posts and strike the right tone and voice for whatever space they're writing in).

Again, the winning approach to take when you're starting out new is to write for free or very low rates. Someone will be willing to take a chance on you if they have a tight budget, or if you're just passionate and knowledgeable about the topic and willing to write for free at first.

If you do a good job, your first clients may even start paying you or raise your pay (if you ask them at the right time). But if not, you can start finding paying clients using the work you've done to provide published writing samples to show you're a proven blogger. Your first clients will mostly likely be happy to let you list them as references as well.

Then you slowly increase your rates as you apply for more and more challenging blog writing jobs. This does take a little time. So it is advisable that you look for blogging jobs in topic areas that you care about and find interesting. If you don't care at all about patio paver stones, don't apply for blogging jobs writing about patio paver stones and patio furniture for outdoor hardscaping companies. You'll procrastinate, hate every minute of the work while you're writing, and eventually give up and quit.

As much as we all would like to have more money in our lives, money is not really motivating. Your best chances for a successful blogging side hustle will be in writing blogs that you would write for no money at all just for the enjoyment of it. Ironically, you'll actually make the most money writing about what you would write about for free.

CHAPTER EIGHT

Flipping Used Books

One time in 2018, I got to talking with a guy in a car dealership who was signing the paperwork for a lease on a new car. He told me he was about to move to another city in my state because his wife was starting her PhD program at a university there.

I asked him what he does, and he told me he flips books for a living. Given what I do for a living, I was naturally intrigued and asked him some more questions about it to learn how he was going about flipping books online and how well he was doing at it. I always love having these conversations with people out and about.

He told me pretty much what I expected. He scouts out Goodwill and other thrift stores, used bookstores, pawn shops, garage sales, and flea markets for used books. When he sees one in good condition that he has a feeling might sell well, he looks it up on Amazon to see what it's going for. If it's selling for more on Amazon than at his used book sources, he buys it and flips it for an easy profit. It's a very straightforward, ridiculously easy to do online side hustle.

I asked him if he'd mind telling me how much he makes at it. He showed me the credit application he was filling out for the financing on the lease and pointed to the space next to gross monthly income. It said $7,000. Flipping books was no online side hustle for this guy. It may have started out that way, but he was now making a far above average income (median income in the US in 2019 was $63,179-- this book flipper was pulling eighty-four geez).

He was working to support himself and his wife with a nice standard of living while saving money for retirement in the distant future while she went through school so she could earn a higher salary after graduating. And he had no boss. No one telling him what to do. No schedule. No deadlines. No meetings. And no stress.

You could tell he wasn't stressed. He didn't have that haggard look of someone suffering from time famine and overwork. Just strolls around used book stores, buys them, takes some photos with his smartphone and lists them online, then puts them in the mail when someone orders one of his books.

Life does not have to be hard. Almost anyone can do this. Almost no one is doing it. Most people are still running whatever dreadful hamster wheel they feel stuck on and won't allow themselves to believe they can do anything else. Even if they're afraid they won't make enough income at something like this, they could start out as a side hustle while keeping their day job. But there's an endless list of alibis and excuses, and Netflix shows to binge.

Tragically and ironically, if they had the kind of freedom this guy has, they could drop everything and binge their favorite show, then get back to buying and flipping used books when it suits their schedule. And it does take some money up front to do this side hustle, but not much. You don't have to buy the whole used book store to start out. A small amount of seed money that you won't miss can get you the first round of inventory, and you can keep reinvesting the profits for more and more inventory. You plant that seed and water it with time and effort, and it'll flourish.

When scouting for used books, checking Amazon and eBay is a good way to see what the general market pricing looks like relative to your local market. But you can also use BookScouter. You just enter the book's ISBN number next to the barcode, and it will compare prices on the book from over 50 vendors. You can also sell it directly to the vendor right from the app. It'll even email you a shipping label with free shipping.

You can also list the book for sale on Amazon and eBay. You have to open an Amazon Seller account to do this. Super easy. And here's a hot tip that not a lot of book flippers are savvy to yet, but I've seen people doing this on Instagram with a lot of success: You can flip use books on Instagram. There are tons of buyers on that platform, with deep pockets, who love books. They specifically follow used book accounts and regularly buy from them. This is a good place to niche, and sell children's books or books of a certain theme. People on Insta love that.

CHAPTER NINE

Online User Testing

One great online side hustle is getting paid to be a guinea pig. A user experience guinea pig, that is. No living in a lab, running hamster wheels, or dealing with border line mad scientist researchers in white lab coats required! Well capitalized tech startup companies and old blue chip corporate giants with massive user facing digital platforms deploy massive amounts of money to get user feedback about their platforms' interface design and user experience.

This has created a ton of opportunities for online side hustlers to make some real coin by signing up for accounts on different tech platforms, using the platform, and giving feedback about their experience: what they liked about it, what they didn't like, what they found confusing or difficult to do, and everything else these companies need to know in order to optimize their interface. This is worth a fortune to businesses with big platforms, or that have raised millions in seed funding to scale to that size. There are several outlets that connect online product testers with companies that pay through the outlet to gather user experience data.

One of these is UserTesting.com. You have to sign up

for an account and take some tests, so there's a little bit of work up front to get set up and approved as an online product tester through their website, but not bad. And once you've gotten set up and approved, users can make as much $60 per completed test through UserTesting.com. Our intelligence shows that on average you'll get paid around $20 per test.

It's actually pretty wild and very fun how they conduct the tests. You go onto one of their clients' websites they provide you with (or download one of their clients' apps) and have UserTesting open for the product test. Then it records your live reactions to the website via audio or video. Instead of just randomly clicking around and having to come up with what to say, UserTesting guides you through the test. It has you complete a set of tasks on the website or app, and you give your live reactions and feedback out loud as you're testing.

Corporations with the resources to do so have conducted this kind of testing for decades using focus groups in the room of an office building. They'd show testers whatever their product was, a new device, a corporate advertising slogan, movie screenings-- and solicit their feedback. Then pay them for their time and the valuable information they could use to make their product more appealing to the market. Now through the magic of online, anyone can take part in this market from a Starbucks or their living room with their feet up on the couch.

Well not everyone, but anyone with a computer, Internet connection, and microphone above the age of 18 who speaks English. To test iPhone, iPad, Android, and Android tablet apps you have to have those products of course. UserTesting pays you through PayPal, and their pay will vary based on the product being tested, your demographics, and your quality rating. Which means the more you use it, and the better the quality of your feedback, the more you can earn per test.

So far the company has conducted 3 million paid product tests for giants like Apple, Microsoft, Twitter, eBay, Facebook, Adobe, and Orbitz.

It's not the only service that pays people to do remote user testing. TryMyUI.com is another in this category. They've served Bose, NBC, Amazon, British Airways, and Priceline among others with live recorded usability tests that they pay testers to do. When you go to their website, you just select "Get Paid To Test" to get started as a product tester. It's similar to UserTesting, and that it uses recorded video of your live reactions to provide feedback. TryMyUI pays $10 per test, and tests take about 20 minutes. So if $30/hour is better than your current rate, this is a sweet side hustle to maximize free time and turn it into cash. One final tip is Userlytics.com. It's a similar service to UserTesting and TryMyUI. They provide paid user testing insights to companies like Microsoft, Google, Philips, L'Oreal, American Airlines, and The Washington Post. Like the other two companies, they record your live reactions as you test online or app interfaces, and testing is available for both PC/Mac and mobile devices. Pay ranges between $5 - $90 depending on different factors and they pay through PayPal.

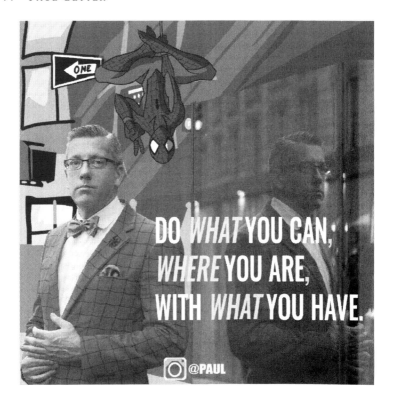

CHAPTER TEN

Teaching English

Those who can do. Those who can't teach! It's a funny joke, but it hurts my feelings because I teach people how to make money online. Oh well, let the haters hate. Teaching is obviously one of the most important and valuable professions in society. In China they revere teachers.

Once I met an economics teacher who takes students on a yearly trip to China in the summer time to learn about international business. He said one day he was passing down the street and overheard someone say something about "foreign devils" in Mandarin. This teacher could speak a fair amount of Mandarin because of his regular visits. He turned to the Chinese guy and said, "Not devil. Teacher." He says the man's entire attitude suddenly changed. And he bowed to the American teacher. Respect.

The great thing about online is anyone who actually can teach is allowed to. You don't have to have a four year degree in education to do online teaching, and make a good side income from it, or even turn it into a full time way to earn a living. You can go Wild West on this and have a lot of success, finding all the best places to post ads offering SAT / ACT tutoring, or give remote piano lessons via webcam, or teach English online. But there are also online platforms that directly connect clients with online teachers, vet and qualify their teachers, provide guidance, and pay you through the platform. VIPKid.com is one such platform for teaching English online to very important Chinese kids. You don't need to know a word of Chinese to get paid to teach English on VIPKid, but of course you do have to be able to speak English well. You don't have to have a college degree in education or English to teach on the platform. You just have to sign up and complete a questionnaire to determine whether you're qualified to teach English to Chinese kids. Then you do a short demo lesson to interview for the gig. Then you do one mock class with a current teacher, and after that you start giving real English lessons.

It's remote work. You can work from anywhere, and it's flexible hours. You choose when you work and how much you work. So it's an ideal side hustle. You teach students one-on-one. The pay is on average $22/hour. So far the platform boasts 100,000 teachers, 700,000 students, and monthly class volumes above 5 million. So there's plenty of steady work.

OnlineEnglishTeaching.com is another platform for getting paid to teach English online. They're actually more like a talent scout / staffing agency for flex workers that connects online side hustlers who want to teach English online with companies that provide this service. You fill out a questionnaire on their website and they match you up with the best company that suits your needs and qualifications.

They place teachers with VIPKid, and also: GoGoKid, SayABC, PalFish, Whales English, Qkids, Cambly, iTutor, Magic Ears, DaDa, Landi, and VIPX. Of course you can also look into any of these yourself if you'd rather do the legwork of finding the best fit, than leave it up to OnlineEnglishTeaching. But they do specialize in doing that part for you to save you time.

Some other companies they don't include are TeachAway.com, 51Talk.com, and EnglishHuntUSA.com. As you can see, there is a massive demand for this work. Enough demand for several big companies in this space. Because it's flexible remote work, it's a perfect online side hustle. But there's also enough opportunity to work these gigs full time and make your living this way.

CHAPTER ELEVEN

Drop Shipping

Say you want to start an online retail business, but you're short on cash. After all, if you were swimming in a sea of money like Scrooge McDuck, you wouldn't need to start the online retail business! But contrary to the old adage, it doesn't always take money to make money. Just a little knowledge, time, and sweat equity (work). Say you want to start a business selling shirts and shoes online, but can't spring for the inventory. Either you don't have the savings, or you don't want to risk your savings on inventory that might not sell. No shirt, no shoes, no problem. Drop shipping is the answer. That's setting up an online store front to sell a product you don't actually have in stock, but that a wholesale distributor does. (Wholesale buys from the manufacturer and sells to retail. Retail sells to the person who uses the product. You would be retail. That's basic merchandising business terminology, but just in case you didn't know, there it is.) Drop shipping is an amazing business model for entrepreneurs because it takes all the risk, hassle, and mess of inventory management out of the equation of retail selling.

When a customer places an order for one of the

products in your store, you forward the order on to the wholesaler. The wholesaler bills you at their wholesale price, and you get paid by your customer at whatever retail price you mark up the product to. No filling your garage or bonus room with inventory and sweating through sleepless nights until it sells.

So to set it up you can use Shopify or Clickfunnels to build a storefront and optimize it with sales copy and images of the product, and a checkout cart so the customer can buy it. Then you run an ad campaign on Google, Facebook, or a thousand other websites to send some traffic there and see if you have a profitable business on your hands. Do your research first before settling on a product to commit a small amount of money to ad testing.

Browse drop shipping company directories like Oberlo, Spocket, Modalyst, and AliExpress for a product to sell. Then look and see what that product or similar ones are selling for on different online retailers' websites. And find out how much it will cost you per clickthrough to your sales page on different ad networks for an ad targeting people who would want to buy the product. Once you've found something that you can reasonably mark up high enough that if 2 - 5% of visitors buy it, they'll cover your ad costs and return a profit, it might be worth a test.

For this reason you want to mark your products up high. Don't be scared. People love to spend money. Sometimes products sell more at higher price points than they do at lower price points. The higher price point signals perceived value. And sometimes it's the packaging that matters. How your website looks and presents the product could make all the difference in conversion.

Niching is important to this game. Say you look and see "bird cages." Okay market them to owners of expensive pet birds like the Hyacinth Macaw. (Make sure the cage is big enough for the bird. Do your research.) Then your website doesn't sell bird cages. It sells Hyacinth Macaw cages. I have no idea what Google Adwords search volume for that is, and if it's a big enough market to make business off of.

But if it's not, do cockatiel cages, or parrot cages. Build value in the sales copy. Ham it up. Tell a story. Help them visualize how happy their bird will be in their cage. Don't just sell the cage package it together with bird toys and mirrors to justify the markup, then drop ship all of it. Let customers know in the follow up email when they make a purchase that they'll get it all in different packages so you don't get worried emails if parts of their order show up a day later than the rest. This is just an example of how to go about it. Apply this thinking as you hunt for ideas, and find something you know and care about to sell. Happy hunting!

CHAPTER TWELVE

Journalism

If you have a flair for writing and you like following news, there are more journalism jobs than ever before in our digital era, and many of them are flexible, remote work freelancing type gigs to build your resume and go full time if you want. You don't just have to follow current events and political news to be a journalist.

Sports journalism is a massively lucrative business. If you're a sports junkie you can get paid to write commentary on the game, or the trade, or the latest fiasco. Entertainment, celebrity, gaming, business, music, tech, health, lifestyle, and music journalism are all places where freelancers can get a foot in the door and start making money online writing about their most avid interest.

One way to go about it is look through the most popular news websites in the niche you're interested in writing for and see if they're hiring writers. Many of them hire freelancers to pump out the headlines and content. Contact the site directly and inquire about writing for them. As with some other side hustles in this book, writing for free or a low rate at first is a good way to get a foot in the door, establish a portfolio of work, and then start charging more.

If the first place that hires you doesn't want to start paying, or raise your pay after you prove your chops, you can leverage the published work you've done for them to apply for another gig and ask for more pay. Here are some good places to look for journalism gigs:

There's always one or two in there that are looking for a remote position and part time work. Search Indeed.com, FlexJobs.com, ZipRecruiter.com, and LinkedIn.com's job postings for "freelance journalism jobs." Include a niche if you have something in particular you're searching to write about. JournalismJobs.com is another good place to look. Upwork.com occasionally has freelance journalism gigs, but you'll probably have to check it regularly for a bit, but you might luck out the first time you check. MediaBistro.com has a good journalism jobs board. For political news, Memeorandum.com has a "Who's Hiring in Media" board on their front page.

News media today is more agile and flexible than it's ever been. That's all thanks to the online revolution. Many news companies don't even have the overhead of a headquarters. Their journalists are freelancers distributed across time zones or continents, working from their laptops in coffee shops and at home. Because of the speed news travels now with social media, they are very fast paced and expect quick turnaround on articles. You'll find breaking news to report on and pitch it to an editor from your computer or phone, then write it if you get approval. Or claim a news tip in a message channel for the journalists and get writing.

The appetite for news on these smart phones is absolutely voracious and growing all the time. Together with social media it's growing into a deeper and more sophisticated ecosystem every day. It needs content all the time to fill all these widening and multiplying channels, and give the chattering classes something to talk about. This is an online side hustle and a potential career for those who love to write, stay current on a popular news beat, and continually feed the beast.

CHAPTER THIRTEEN

Amazon eBooks

Here's one that's more time intensive up front with less guarantee of a payoff. But if you're good at writing, knowledgeable about a topic that helps people (or willing to become knowledgeable about it to write a solid eBook), and self-motivated to see it through, this is a great source of side income for a lot of people. Many others make a living this way.

Writing eBooks and self-publishing them on Amazon KDP (Kindle Direct Publishing) is a very approachable way to make money working from home on your laptop. It may seem like a daunting task to write a book, but that's a defense-against-change mechanism many people have to keep them from ever starting on something they dream of. Who doesn't know someone who really wants to write a book, mentions their dream every so often, but never does?

There's something completely relatable about that reverence for the written word, but it doesn't have to be this monumental task many build it up in their mind to be. To begin with, you do not have to write a 250 page book to sell eBooks on Amazon and other self publishing platforms like Barnes and Noble, iBooks, and Smashword. In fact you will have a tougher time selling an eBook of that length than selling a shorter eBook. Aim for a book that's just 6,000 - 10,000 words. People are more likely to buy a book that doesn't take too long to read, and that's the sweet spot for selling a lot of eBooks on Amazon and other similar platforms. The price point is another part to keep as accessible to a general audience as possible. $2.99 is an ideal price to go for volume. Price any higher and a lot of people will buy a competing eBook, or if it's in a non-fiction genre, they'll just go read some free blog posts on the topic recommended by Google.

As for how to pick your topic, here's a big tip: eBooks that help people solve a problem are big sellers on Amazon. So brainstorm a list of books you would like to write (and for which you might be able to create something really useful) that you could title starting with the words "How to." That's a great approach to create some of the most lucrative eBooks. Now if you're a creative person, and can write some great stories, by all means write short stories in the recommended word range, and string them together as serials for a nice side hustle.

There are a lot of romance, mystery, and science fiction writers making a living pumping out eBook fiction in these genres. But it is a content grind, not usually a path to mailbox millions off a smash hit. To do this side hustle you really have to enjoy writing. Whether you go with fiction, non-fiction, or both, after brainstorming topics to get started, do a ton of research on Amazon's bestsellers based on the first list you brainstorm. Then go back and brainstorm again, using what you've learned from seeing what sells.

While you're doing this research, pay close attention to the titles, cover art, and the descriptions. Those have more to do with how many copies your eBook will sell than what's actually in the eBook! When you've finished writing the book, pay an actual graphic designer on Fivrr to make the cover for you. Give them three examples of the best selling books in your topic area or adjacent to your topic to use as references. This is really important. Do not do your cover yourself if you are not a professional graphic designer or graphic design side hustler.

You can write the eBook in any word processor and export it into the correct format to upload to Amazon. For all of Amazon Kindle's formatting rules and best practices, go to http://kdp.amazon.com. They tell you exactly what to do, step-by-step to format your eBook correctly and upload it to be listed on the Amazon Kindle marketplace. They also tell you the dimensions and guidelines for cover art, so forward those requirements to your graphic designer. Don't assume they'll know.

Now you'll be faced with a decision when you upload your eBook to Amazon. You can enroll it in Amazon's KDP Select program to make more money. Your book has to meet a couple basic requirements for this, but the main thing is you can't offer it for sale anywhere else. On the upside in this program, Kindle subscribers who pay a fee to "borrow" as many books as they'd like can borrow your book and you get paid a certain amount for every page they read. On the other hand, you miss out on Barnes and Noble, iBooks, and Smashword. It might be worth testing a book each way to see what nets you the most profit.

CHAPTER FOURTEEN

Patreon

Patreon is a perfect example of how the Internet has fundamentally changed how the world economy works. Economics and business used to be directly transactional. It was all about having something that someone else wanted, and charging them as much for it as you possibly could, so as to extract the most resources possible out of others.

Before, if someone couldn't pay, they didn't get the goods. And the absolute best players at this game were the ones who cornered the market for something and made off like Mr. Money Bags off the cover of the Monopoly box. It's not like that any more. Well at least it's less like that than ever before.

Now we live in the attention economy, and the gift economy. It's something made possible because of the Internet. And as the Internet continues to scale to cosmic proportions, the gift economy is growing to make up a greater and greater share of the world economy.

Patreon is a subscription donation platform for online content creators. Think of it like a Kickstarter, but with one important difference: Kickstarter is for raising a round of funds one time to launch a product. But Patreon is for getting paid monthly subscribers who pay you a certain amount every month for free content you produce online. Patreon is all about the gift economy. It's for creators who give away their online goods for free instead of hiding it behind a paywall and requiring people to pay in order to read it, watch it, listen to it, play it or use it. And it's for fans and users who choose to make a gift of their monthly subscription anyway, voluntarily, even though the goods are already free.

And a lot of people are making a solid living or running a nice side hustle using Patreon to monetize their podcast, their YouTube channel, their Twitch stream, their blog, their art, their music, their app, their snaps, their tweets, or any number of other online goods that are distributed digitally.

This is not a side hustle for fast cash like some of the others described in this book. It's one for someone who doesn't need to make income quickly, who already makes enough income from their main hustle, and who has some free time they'd like to devote to a hobby they love and hopefully begin to monetize it after building a following.

The upside for someone in the position to do a side hustle like this is they have the opportunity to do something they really love more than anything and have an endless amount of passion and ideas for. It could take a year or years of consistent effort to get your Patreon to start paying out some pretty coin, but for those who have the time and a passion, it's a nice long term strategy for achieving your destiny in the digital world.

So to begin this side hustle you need to produce something consistently to distribute for free online and begin to build a following. After you've set up whatever your hustle is, you start a Patreon and let your fans or users know you've got one. Remind them gently every so often about it. Don't be pushy or obnoxious about promoting your Patreon. Just let them know it's there and your true fans will begin to contribute.

Patreon lets you set up different "Tiers" with different monthly donation amounts. For each higher tier, you offer an increasingly nicer reward to patrons as an incentive to sign up. I recommend you don't get bogged down in this, especially as you're just starting out.

Setting up five different donation tiers from $5 to $100 will get you nowhere fast. Your fans will be just as unsure of which tier to pick as you will be of how what rewards to give for each (you can waste an enormous amount of time overthinking this). Instead set just two tiers. Make them $1 and $2. Then make the reward something simple that's easy for you to fulfill.

Good rewards are usually some kind of product upgrade / bonus like exclusive content for patrons only. Or a monthly live stream Q&A with patrons only. Be sure to add a nice photo for your Patreon page and good description. Fill everything out. Don't leave anything blank. But also don't take forever to do it and overthink it.

CHAPTER FIFTEEN

YouTube

Video killed the radio star. And YouTube minted a million video stars. (Ironically many of them are musicians who use the platform to promote their music and music videos.) We are far from peak YouTube. YouTube has over 2 billion active monthly users, 30 million active daily users, and a staggering 1 billion hours worth of viewing every day spread out over 5 billion videos a day. It's unreal what an absolute cosmic ocean of video this platform is.

How well does it monetize using the native YouTube ads? It depends on the content your channel covers. It's well known that different topics are more profitable advertising niches than others. If your channel is about underwater basket weaving or how to plant turnips out of season, you might not monetize as well as a channel about gaming, electronics, photography, personal finance, or something with a large market of people who spend a lot of money on related products. Keep that in mind as you pick a niche, but remember money isn't everything and you'll make nothing but headaches doing a channel about something you don't actually care about, but think it might make a lot of money.

Now to give you the more direct answer: On average a YouTube channel will make anywhere from $2 - $5 per 1,000 views, or $2,000 - $5,000 per 1,000,000. Before you start mentally cashing those checks and getting excited about finally having a girlfriend now, know it is very hard to get even 1,000 views on a video. Even getting your first 100 views is tough unless you already have a huge online following and branch out to YouTube from another platform where you're doing well.

So this is another side hustle that's more hobby that could make money if you stick with it consistently for three years than a way to start pulling in gas and grocery money next week. For those kind of money making opportunities, stick with hustles like Upwork, Steady, or teaching English online. But if you got the time and passion, and would do it for free anyways just for fun, there are a lot of people in the world making more than their parents did playing video games and uploading the video of themselves playing and their screen capture to YouTube.

But all of them were doing it as a hobby for the love of what they were doing for months or even years before they started seeing any kind of money to speak of. PewDiePie, the king of gaming YouTube, and most subscribed channel for years, was working in a hot dog stand to pay the bills for years while making YouTube videos of himself playing Minecraft just for fun. His friend, JackScepticEye, another YouTube millionaire, was living in his parents' house for free.

Obviously some basic requirements for this side hustle are a camera that films reasonably high quality video, a basic Google search of proper lighting, and a strong camera presence. YouTube is about entertainment even when it's about informing viewers. If you are shy, quiet, or boring, you will have a tough time on YouTube.

Either don't even try this, or change to become confident, loud, and interesting-- at least for the camera.

You will also need to research how to write headlines that people can't resist clicking and use what you learn to write every headline. And what thumbnails people can' resist clicking to use what you learn for every video thumbnail. Tagging and keywords in the description must also be done with knowledge and care. Above all if your goal is to eventually get a large audience and begin making money, you have to upload a new video every day. Plain and simple, YouTube's algorithm rewards channels that upload daily. They want to draw users toward channels that will continue creating more content for them to watch so they'll subscribe and come back for more each day. This is a hustle you have to know you're going to be able to devote an hour a day to making a video, editing it, and uploading it. Every day. Forever. Otherwise your channel will never make more than a few pennies.

CHAPTER SIXTEEN

Twitch

You can probably just skip this side hustle if you're not addicted to video games. But if you do waste three hours a day playing video games, and you spend a truly stupid amount of money on new consoles, games, loot boxes, graphics cards, gaming chairs, snacks-- well then you obviously have a serious problem. A super fun, serious problem. And if you have a gaming problem, you absolutely should turn it into a money making solution and make a side hustle out of it. Then your habit could at least pay for itself, or maybe even pay some other bills too.

It is truly amazing to be alive and kicking this deep into the 21st Century. Growing up playing video games was looked down upon by all of society as a complete waste of time. Worse, our parents and teachers, pretty much everybody told us that playing video games was rotting our minds and making us stupid. Little did the naysayers know that science would eventually find playing video games actually enhances our creativity and problem solving skills. Even better, kids are becoming millionaires playing video games and streaming it on Twitch.

That is a truly sweet "Revenge of the Nerds" scenario. As the old Klingon proverb goes: "Revenge is a dish best served cold." As in cold, hard cash from something everyone told you was an embarrassing waste of your life. Now don't get too excited. This side hustle is like YouTube in that income will build very slowly, and only if you have a likeable, interesting personality, and consistently stream at least three times a week.

Twitch is a live streaming site mostly used by gamers to watch other gamers play video games and comment. Some Twitch streams are more serious. They're about analyzing the game play and offering viewers commentary about how to improve at the game. Others are more comedic, they're just about goofing off and having fun while playing. People watching get the feeling they're sitting next to their friend at home playing video games together in real life. Some streams are a mix between the two.

The way you make money on Twitch is by gathering a large following of people who tune in to watch your broadcasts. Then you monetize it by applying to be a Twitch Affiliate once you meet certain requirements and get paid by the company every time you stream. The top 1% of streamers graduate to become Twitch Partners, and get a number of benefits in addition to even more distribution, growing their stream faster. But there are other ways to make money on Twitch outside the official channels. Many streamers with large followings monetize by posting affiliate links to their Twitch page. In case you didn't know, these are links to products for sale that pay out a small commission when someone clicks the link and buys the product. Amazon affiliate links are the most common on Twitch. In addition to affiliate links, streamers also arrange sponsorships with companies to mention their product on their stream and get paid. Just be sure you disclose anything you get paid to promote is a paid promotion so you say in line with terms of service and FTC regulations. Some streamers also have Patreons that their most devoted fans chip in some money to every month to keep the stream going. If you're very good at gaming, like incredibly competitive at it, then playing in tournaments and streaming is another way to make money from any tourney winnings in addition sponsorships and affiliate ads. If you're this good, you might even develop a fandom and be able to sell merch as well.

CHAPTER SEVENTEEN

Fiverr

Fiverr is another massive clearinghouse platform like Upwork. It connects freelance flex workers in the digital economy to clients who need a project done. Don't let the name fool you. It originally started as a website where all projects were five dollars, but quickly changed and allowed freelancers to set whatever prices they want when they discovered asking people to work for just five dollars made everybody hate them. (They even got an "F" from the Better Business Bureau. But they did turn things around and now have a "B.")

There are many people making a part time, full time, and deep six figure income on these platforms. In June 2018, CNBC featured a young woman who quit her job at a public relations firm in 2016 because she couldn't stand working there any longer. She started taking freelance jobs on Fiverr.

That year she made $33,000 dollars hustling. The next year she grossed $81,000. And the year CNBC did the story about her, she had already made $150,000 and it was only June. She had worked her way up to a very nice, above average income in less than three years.

There are a few important differences between Fiverr

and Upwork. The most important one is that Upwork features job postings that freelancers with the necessary skills apply to. On Fiverr it works in reverse. Freelancers post services they offer packaged into different deals, and clients browse the listings to hire a freelancer whose services they need.

Either way you will have to market yourself and your skills, but Fiverr will require some more work up front to create and really polish not only your freelancers profile, but the services and packages you offer. One great way freelancers earn more money on Fiverr is by offering different tiers of the same service with fewer or more options and commensurate pricing.

Succeeding on Fiverr is the same game as success on Upwork. You have to start out small, humble, and hungry. The first month or so on the platform you have to eat like a bird and poop like an elephant. Pardon my French. Bid your services low to attract some clients who are willing to take a risk on a new freelancer because they're on a budget and you do a good job of selling yourself and your services.

Then as you rack up completed jobs and excellent ratings, you can start raising your rates and continue to get new clients. It's a snowball effect. But be sure you do get those excellent ratings. It's hard to come back from a bad review on a reputation-driven marketplace where the client doesn't know you from Adam and only has previous clients' ratings to go off of.

That means being polite, professional, and prompt. Communicate clearly, have a positive, cheerful, helpful attitude in all your communications with clients, and put in overtime to make the work you do stand out. Turn in work that you're really proud of and that you know the client is going to be very happy with. Then be sure to ask for a good rating by specifically asking the client if there's any reason they can think of that they couldn't give you a perfect rating. Continue to maintain this attitude and working process until you get old and retire or die. It will serve you well at anything you do in life. But you can continue to iterate this attitude and process on Fiverr or Upwork to leverage your present work into higher paying future work, again and again. Especially as you increase your experience and skill level at the work you're doing. Who knows what the limit on this might be for you.

The one lady making $150,000 in six months was editing high level government documents and personal text messages from a member of the British royal family who wanted a professional to take a look before hitting send.

CHAPTER EIGHTEEN

Copywriting

Think you've got what it takes to write copy as a side hustle? Copywriting (not copyrighting, this isn't registering for trademarks) is writing the text (copy) in advertisements, publicity materials, marketing campaigns, email list newsletters, and sales pages. It's very lucrative work.

A brand new, inexperienced online copywriter just starting out from scratch can pick up an extra $300 to $1500 a month writing copy online depending on their basic aptitude (you have to already be good at writing) and how much time and effort they put into it. An experienced copywriter doing it for a living can make a comfortable, above-average US income writing copy. The most highly paid copywriting professionals make hundreds of thousands of dollars a year writing copy.

The reason copywriting is so valuable is it's sales translated into the written medium. And sales is one of the most valuable parts of any business. It's so valuable, the sales department is the surest route to CEO of most big companies, followed by accounting since taming and maximizing a company's financials is pretty key. And the poor product guys, forget about them. iMac, iPhone, and iPod designer Jony Ives didn't become CEO of Apple when Steve Jobs died. Salesperson Tim Cook did. The value of writing marketing and sales focused copy is amplified in the digital online era, wherein so many prospect interactions with a company are copy based, not face to face as in the brick and mortar days of yore. There are more channels than ever for copy that need to be filled with well written business talk. And in the hyper-competition of today's digital marketplace, the ones who are best at it end up with very lucrative careers.

So this is a side hustle, yes, but it's another one in this book with basically endless potential for the right person who brings their A-game to it and pours their time and energy into it. But it doesn't have to be that for you either, if all you're looking for is a good side hustle. There's plenty of cream for you skim off the top.

The best strategy for copywriting is pick a niche to specialize in. Find a large, healthy industry that you're interested in and care about, and write copy for that industry. Find clients on Upwork, Fiverr, Freelancer.com, Guru.com, and ProBlogger.com. Use the same strategy described in the chapters on Upwork, Fiverr, and website design. Bid low at first and build up your book of business with solid work every step up along the way.

You can also niche the kind of copywriting you do as well as the industry you write in. That's another winning strategy. For instance, some copywriters excel at search engine optimization (SEO). They write web page copy and optimize the URL, page title, search engine headline, search meta description, subheadings, text, image alt text, and more to increase the likelihood that the web page ranks high on search engine results pages for certain search terms.

Other copywriting niches include business blogging,

email newsletter copywriting, social media marketing, sales and squeeze page writing (get good at this and you can do amazing things with ClickFunnels), product descriptions, resumes, and plenty more niches I can't think of off the top of my head at the moment. You might end up dabbling in or specializing in more than one of these niches as your side hustle grows.

The important thing to bear in mind if you build a copywriting side hustle, is be sure to spend 90% of your time getting clients and doing the work, and 10% of your side hustling time reading up on copywriting to learn how to sharpen your skills from the very best. Actually even if you just devote 5% of your side hustle time to this, it will put you head and shoulders above 99% of the new freelancers like you just getting started out in this field.

CHAPTER NINETEEN

Data Entry

If you're not a record keeping or numbers nerd, you might want to skip this chapter. No sense doing a side hustle that's going to give you a headache. But if you are savvy with the math or love to keep records, and enjoy working with numbers or spreadsheets, you can get a good online side hustle going in data entry. It's pretty basic, straightforward work. Cool thing too for math based data entry is it's a stepping stone for some to very high paying careers in data analytics

These kinds of jobs are at the forefront of telecommuting work because they can be done from anywhere in the world. The company doesn't need its data engineers in any specific location. They just need someone to look at the numbers in their computers and do stuff with those numbers. Yeah I know, "do stuff" is a highly technical data science term.

But the point is these are the kind of jobs people can do from their laptop while at home several time zones away, or traveling up and down the West coast in a trailer and working out of Starbucks' and Paneras, or from where ever in the world you'd like to live, not because you have a job there, but just because that's where you want to live. Wake up and smell the freedom.

Data entry is a varied field and encompasses a number of different jobs. But they all involve entering data of some kind into a system of some kind. That might be clerical work making written records of something in a system. Or it could be numeral, entering values or codes into a spreadsheet. It could be transcription work from photo-scanned documents into a digital record.

For example, a data entry job might involve going through an endless digital stack of photo-scanned client records, then referring to a spreadsheet and making sure the address in the spreadsheet is consistent with what's on the photo-scanned record, and marking it correct in the system if it is, or correcting it and notating in the system that you made a correction. People of a certain temperament enjoy this kind of work, while people with another kind of temperament find it tedious. But if you are the kind of person who likes to be meticulous, and keep things orderly, data entry might be for you. There is a certain pleasantly relaxing quality to the flow of data entry work. You can put on music or listen to books on audiotape as you do any of the entry level work.

Best place to go for data entry gigs is Upwork. Fiverr also offers these services to its clients under its programming and tech category. Truelancer.com is another one you can try to find data entry work. PeoplePerHour.com has new data entry job listings every day. Freelancer.com also has data entry work. You can also search Indeed.com and ZipRecruiter.com for remote work data entry jobs and there's always a lot to find there.

KEEP YOUR THOUGHTS POSITIVE
because your thoughts become your words.

KEEP YOUR WORDS POSITIVE
because your words become behavior.

KEEP YOUR BEHAVIOR POSITIVE
because your behavior become your habits.

KEEP YOUR HABITS POSITIVE
because your habits become your values.

KEEP YOUR VALUES POSITIVE
because your values become your destiny.

CHAPTER TWENTY

eBay / Amazon Flipping

Books aren't the only great product to flip online for a nice side hustle. You can flip any number of used and new goods and sell them on eBay or Amazon at a markup for profit. The technical business or economic term for it is retail arbitrage. Arbitrage is a fancy word for buying something in a cheaper market to resell it in a more expensive market at a profit.

As they say on Wall Street, "Buy low! Sell high!" In essence, that's all flipping goods on eBay and Amazon is-- finding a product you can buy low and sell high. There's no guesswork involved in this game either. That's the beauty of it. You can go through a garage sale or a clearance rack in a retail store, find something that catches your eye, and look it up on eBay and Amazon to see what it's selling for. If it's selling for significantly more than what you can buy it for on the spot, bingo. You've got a product worth flipping.

There are now a number of apps that take even more of the guesswork out of retail arbitrage. If you want to flip goods for a side hustle, some apps worth trying are: Profit Bandit, ScanPower, Scoutify, and Amazon Seller.

With Profit Bandit, all you have to do is walk into a

store with a sale going on, scan a barcode with your phone, and it will tell you how much profit you can make by reselling it on Amazon. The app boasts a "built-in profit calculator to provide the most accurate profit figure, including postage rates and FBA fees." FBA stands for Fulfillment by Amazon. You send the product to Amazon and they fulfill the order for you. Profit Bandit is a very feature rich app with a number of functionalities to help support an Amazon arbitrage retailer.

ScanPower is similar. When you scan an item's barcode, ScanPower will display the item's 5 lowest New, Used, and FBA offers on Amazon. Scoutify is another app that provides flipping people with information about the current market pricing and potential profitability of an item they're scouting out to flip. Now Amazon Seller is unlike the three apps mentioned above. It doesn't service flippers with information about potential ROI when they're out scouting for goods to buy and resell. Amazon Seller helps you, "Analyze your sales, fulfill orders, find products to sell, manage offers, inventory and returns, and quickly respond to customer questions." It provides inventory, order, and return management. It's very robust. You can run a business from your phone with this app.

Another way these flipping people appraise the potential resell value of a good is using a website called Camel Camel Camel. Creatively enough, their website can be accessed by pointing your browser at CamelCamelCamel.com. It helps you find the current market pricing and sales ranking of items your scouting. As for where to go on scouting raids, garage sales, thrift stores, and flea markets are ideal for used goods. You can find some real diamonds in the rough. It's a little tougher without the retail barcode you can use the apps above to scan when scouting new goods. But with a little knowledge about what you're scouting, you can find some treasures at ridiculously steep discounts that are flippable for a huge profit.

For selling new goods, see what's on clearance at Walmart, Target, Meijer, Home Depot, Lowes, Kroger, Menards, Bed Bath & Beyond, Office Depot, and Staples. When these places have inventory eating up the floor plan without moving, they mark it down and let it go. That's your opportunity to resell it at a higher price on Amazon and eBay for some side hustle money.

That's right. People are selling Walmart's market down goods on Amazon for profit and making side money and even a good living that way. You can also use apps like Groupon, Raise, Discount Stores, and Retail Me Not to find deals on goods in your area.

CHAPTER TWENTY-ONE

Day Trading

Most of the side hustles in this book range on a spectrum from low risk / quick payday to high risk / long leadtime. But day trading is different. It's high risk / quick payday (possibly, hence the high risk part). Day trading used to be the sole domain of Wall Street boiler rooms with Gordon Gekko types taking advantage of state of the art computer equipment and privileged access to market news and financial information. Now that the Internet has democratized everything, it's democratized day trading as well.

Today the rest of us who don't work in office buildings in Manhattan have just as near instant access to information from the phones on our hips as anyone else. And a number of commission free brokerage apps to buy and sell stocks and other securities has opened up day trading to the retail investor. Top it all off with an entirely new class of securities that didn't exist before, with a total market capitalization of more than $300 billion in 2020: cryptocurrency. The time is ripe for day trading as an online side hustle.

Day traders buy and sell securities like stocks, bonds, ETFs, futures, and cryptocurrencies. The goal is to buy securities at a bargain when their price is lower than you expect it will be in the near future, and sell them at a profit when their price is higher. Then use your profits to repeat the process again and again. Even successful day traders take losses on some of their trades, but their winnings make enough to cover their losses and take home a profit.

When just starting out, you may want to use an app with no fees for trades like Robinhood or Cash App. Just bear in mind that both of these apps do restrict you to three day trades (buying and selling an asset within the same day) over a rolling five day period. That's okay. You may not want to make very many intra-day trades. Robinhood lifts this limit once you have a $25,000 cash balance. If you get the point of making more day trades than these apps allow, you can also use the TD Ameritrade and E*TRADE apps, but they do charge $6.95 per trade.

If you're worried about risk, or you want to learn how some of the best traders make money, download the eToro app. It's almost like social media day trading. You can follow other users' trades and see how much money they're making. In 2019 they even introduced a new feature called "Copytrading." It lets you pick a user who has a solid track record of making money, and devote a certain amount of funds to copy all their positions and trades.

Cryptocurrency is a favorite new sector for day traders because cryptos are very volatile. Their prices swing up and down wildly. So it's a day trader's paradise. Binance is the most high volume cryptocurrency exchange with the most different cryptos trading pairs listed, so it's the best app to use for day trading cryptocurrency.

This side hustle is not for the faint of heart, nor for someone who doesn't do a great deal of research to understand what they're doing. You'll want to familiarize yourself with technical analysis, which is how to read price charts to anticipate future movements. And whatever securities you buy, you'll need to closely follow the news about a company's stock you have a position in or a cryptocurrency you're thinking about going long on. It's a lot of work, but for some people a lot of fun. And it's certainly a high-risk / high-reward side hustle.

CHAPTER TWENTY-TWO

Fitness Influencer

Actually getting paid to stay fit and help others get and stay fit too sounds like an absolute dream, but it's a reality for many people in the online world of today. Not long ago almost no one but athletes exercised, but today staying fit is a high priority for millions and millions of people.

These days even nerds lift weights. For information and inspiration to get fit, people go online, and find fitness influencers. Many people make a living at it, others just get paid for their gym time. Either way it's a sweet hustle. And it'll help you stay healthy and live longer too.

This is an online side hustle that may take time to build up to the point of making income, but if you don't need the money right away, and you have the time and passion for it, this can be a very rewarding side hustle, and a really great way to improve yourself, improve the world, and make money too. That level of convergence of self, community, and prosperity is very ideal.

If you're going to make it as a fitness influencer, it's probably going to be on Instagram. The best way to go about it is start uploading videos and photos of yourself exercising, and of meal prep, along with helpful information about the exercises you do and nutrition. You'll begin to gain a following if you do this consistently and be seen as an authority on health and fitness.

You may want to go for a niche that plays to your own strengths and interests. For instance you might be all about bulking up and bodybuilding. Or you might be about losing wait, staying trim, and getting a flat tummy. Or you may be all about building that super sixpack that everyone wants to have these days. Or you might be about running marathons and cardio, heart health and how to stave off cancer and diabetes to live longer.

Or you might be about CrossFit. Or strength and endurance training. Or yoga, pilates, and meditation. Whatever it is, finding a niche is usually a good way to go because it defines and differentiates you, and people are often interested in fitness with a particular goal in mind, not just general fitness as a concept. Hashtag your posts according to your niche.

As you build up a following on Instagram and establish yourself as an authority in your fitness niche, the most direct path to making money from it, especially with a smaller number of followers, is becoming a remote coach or online fitness trainer. With just a handful of clients you can get a very healthy side hustle going.

Start advertising to your followers that you're offering fitness coaching, and make special offers like a flash sale with discounts on their first six months of coaching, or their first two coaching sessions free. Skype with new clients and ask them about their fitness goals and challenges, and listen to them, then help them make a personal fitness plan tailored to them and explain how you'll help them remain consistent and achieve their goals.

If you're not currently very fit yourself even better. It might take even more time to get to the point of earning from this side hustle, but if getting fit is your goal anyways, with or without the extra income, start posting everything about your progress to Instagram. When you get into the best fitness of your life, that Before / After photo is powerful proof that you can help others transform too, because you already did it yourself.

Fitness influencers that reach a certain level of followers start making money from sponsorships and affiliate ads for equipment, nutritional supplements, food, and athleisure apparel. Once you're doing this well, you can probably make the leap and go full time. Then you'll be making a living just from staying healthy and helping others stay healthy too.

CHAPTER TWENTY-THREE

ClickBank

Say you read the chapter on info products and you like the economics of it. No physical inventory. Infinite digital distribution with no additional marginal cost per unit delivered. But you thinking up and creating a truly professional info product that someone would actually want to buy seems like an impossibly daunting task. Or if you're really honest with yourself, you know you could probably make something pretty good, but you just won't because it's too much work to put together. And the whole time you'll be haunted by the nagging worry that it won't pay off and all your time and effort will be wasted on an info product that no one will buy.

These are valid concerns. It's absolutely better to know this ahead of time and quit before you start, than pull the plug halfway into a project. Also, there's a way to take advantage of the economics of info products without making an info product yourself. ClickBank is a repository of hundreds of hot info products that someone else already made, that sell very well, for affiliate markets to sell and get a commission for every sale they make.

Visit ClickBank.com and click affiliate marketplace

to browse the product offerings. There's some absolute gold there. It's subdivided by categories like: Betting Systems, Business / Investing, Computers / Internet, E-Business & E-Marketing, Education, Employment & Jobs, Fiction, Games, Health & Fitness, Languages, Self-Help, Sports, Travel, and more.

When you click on each product from the Affiliate Marketplace, it will tell you the product's stats: how well it sells, the commission percentage, sometimes how much total commission the product has paid out. Some of these have paid out hundreds of thousands of dollars in commissions. Many of the commission percentages are extremely generous like 60% of the retail sale price of the product. By contrast, Amazon's average affiliate commission percentage is somewhere between 5% and 30% depending on a number of factors.

So with ClickBank, you can find ready made info products with a track record of solid sales, and sell them yourself. If you don't already have a big following online, you'll have to buy traffic by placing ads, and get the traffic to visit a web page you set up (like a ClickFunnels page or a page you set up yourself using any number of other services like Wix, Weebly, etc.).

You pitch the product on the sales page that you direct traffic to from the ad, and place your affiliate link for them to buy so it can track sales and deliver you commissions. Your ad and sales page need to be consistent with each other in messaging and feel. Don't use clickbait in the ad just to drive more traffic. That will get you unqualified traffic that doesn't convert as well and waste your ad dollars.

Experiment with advertising on Facebook, Google, Instagram, Twitter, Reddit, SnapChat, LinkedIn, or any other platform you use a lot and understand well that has paid advertising. Stick with what you know at first. You'll do a better job of designing the ad to fit in with the platform's culture. Each platform has its own culture of course. This side hustle involves risking some money to place ads, but you don't have to front much cash to test out an info product, ad campaign, and sales funnel and see if you've got a hit. The beauty of info products is people spend a lot on them, and it's almost all profit, so you have a wide margin to pay for ads and get a profit from the 5-10+% of visitors that actually buy.

CHAPTER TWENTY-FOUR

Graphic Design

Graphic design is an always in demand, technical skill. Hello, job security. The beauty of it too is that this is work that people can do as a full time job for an agency or big company with in house graphics designers; or as a full time freelancer making a living as their own boss; or as a part time freelancer working an online side hustle. Breaking into it is easy enough if you have the skills.

If you don't have the skills, but you're sure you have the aptitude and would be interested in getting good at graphic design, it's easy to learn from home without having to go to school for it. You don't need a four year degree for this. People don't care about that anymore, especially not for something like graphic design. They just want the job done by whoever has the ability to do it, and can prove it with some samples and a portfolio of the work they've done.

To learn graphic design, you'll need to download Photoshop. The basic version is Elements, and it will only set you back $99.99. It is powerful enough to start with and even run a lucrative side hustle using just Elements alone to get the job done.

Skillshare.com and Coursera.com have plenty of free graphic design and Photoshop courses. You can also find very low cost (like $12) graphic design intro courses on Udemy.com. YouTube is also an absolute goldmine of free Photoshop tutorials. Take a few of these and you'll be a professional in no time.

To get graphics design clients, use all the freelancer / client clearinghouses mentioned in some of the other chapters and others specifically for graphic designers: Upwork, Fiverr, Freelancer.com, DesignPickle.com, 99Designs.com, and DesignHill.com.

Also use the strategy described in the other chapters. Start your rates low so you can get that first client to bite without any previous work experience. Have a couple samples that you've made without a client just to show what you can do. Keep your pitches short and to the point, and exude energy, positivity, and a can do attitude.

Do a phenomenal job and let your client know you'll be happy to rework any submissions if they're not completely satisfied. After you've completed the project, ask them if they're completely satisfied and if there's any reason you can think of that they wouldn't leave you a perfect rating and strong review. Tell them you want to be sure they're 100% happy with your work before they rate you. As you build up a reputation on these platforms and the experience to go for more ambitious projects, you'll be able to steadily raise your rates and take on more clients. You may eventually get to the point where you have more clients than you can handle, and then you can raise your rates just to keep half the world from knocking down your door.

Continue to hone your skills by taking more advanced courses and tutorials, and getting better tooling (more feature rich versions of Photoshop). You may eventually even want to get more physical equipment if this hustle is really bustling, like a Wacom tablet that allows you to use Photoshop with an electronic pen on a screen to freehand draw some of your graphic designs.

CHAPTER TWENTY-FIVE

Inbound / Outbound Calling

Some people just love to talk for hours on the phone. Why not get paid to do it? If you have a pleasant voice and you're good on the phone, you might try inbound / outbound calling as a side hustle. Why get a part time job somewhere with a uniform and a silly hat when you could be in your jammies with Tweety bird house slippers on kicked up on the couch, sipping on a cup of coffee and just calling people? It's a no brainer really.

You can find an endless amount of inbound / outbound calling gigs on freelance websites like Upwork. For an inbound gig, the client sets their system up to forward inbound calls to your phone, and when it rings you answer and follow a certain script the client provides. You'll probably be logged in to some kind of Customer Relationship Management system with an account the client sets up for you, and you log the call and make notes.

It might be customer service inbound. So people call with questions or complaints, and you have a set of scripts to follow that cover all the major categories of phone calls you're going to handle. And if nothing fits any of the scripts, then there's a script for that too, that involves forwarding on the customer to someone else who will be able to handle their issue. You might create a ticket from their call that gets forwarded from the CRM to another department to handle a problem a customer has.

There's also inbound sales. You might take calls from people that want to order a product or schedule an appointment, and you handle the order and mark it in the system. There's also outbound sales, where you make cold, warm, or qualified calls to lists the client provides and follow a script to get a certain kind of conversion. They make a sale, they sign up for something, they make an appointment. Or you might do outbound customer service where you call current clients and say, "Hi, ABC Partners Inc. calling on behalf of your rep at ABC company. Just wanted to make sure everything's going well with your subscription."

Another good website specifically devoted to outbound call freelancers is UpCall.com. You sign up, get approved within a few days, and log in and start making outbound phone calls for their clients for $12/hour. They've served companies like AirBNB, LG, Coldwell Banker, Y Combinator, Farmer's Insurance, and Intuit Quickbooks.

CHAPTER TWENTY-SIX

App Developer

What if there's *not* an app for that? Well an app developer can create one. Learning how to develop apps is a skill that will serve you for the rest of your life in our increasingly digital world. If you're good with computers in 2020 you are amazingly powerful. Gandalf the Grey level powerful. There will be no end to the amount of work there will be for you to do if you learn to develop apps, and potentially no limit to the amount of income you can make from it.

It's something great to do as a side hustle just to get started, but a lot of app developers' side hustles turned into multi-billion dollar platforms like Twitter and Facebook. That's no guarantee that yours will, and it probably won't in all likelihood, but worst case scenario, you learn a lot making things that improve the world somehow and make some money on the side doing it.

If you don't think you can, you might be right, but you seriously might be wrong. Developing an app is a simple matter of learning another language. In the case of app development, the two main languages are Java (for Android apps) and Swift (for Apple apps).

You can't just tell a computer in English: "I'd like for

you to display a screen with three buttons. When the user clicks the first button, I want you to play Mariachi band music. When they click the second button, I want you to email everyone in their contacts list a link to the Wikipedia page about the Muppet Babies. When they click the third button, I want you to display the classic starfield screensaver from Windows '95." But basically that's all programming is, just using a language that translates between English and the computer's ultimate language that consists of ones and zeros. So you just have to learn that intermediary language and you're an instant nerd. To learn either Java or Swift, try CodeAcademy.com. They have a free service and a premium service for $19.99, and you can try out the pro version for free at first to see if it's worth it.

This side hustle is a time intensive one without a quick payday. It's one of the passion hustles that's about developing a skill doing something interesting to you in hope of a not too distant future reward. The most likely path to income from an app is creating a free version with ads and in app purchases, and a premium version with no ads and added features.

What kind of app to create is impossible to tell you because there are an infinite number of possibilities. The best kind of app to create, that you'll have the most fun making, and that will stand the great chance of being profitable, is an app that you would use yourself, an app that you wish existed but doesn't yet. Or a version of other apps that exist, but that bug you because they don't do whatever it is they're supposed to do as well as you think they could.

CHAPTER TWENTY-SEVEN

Domain Flipping

Domain names are online real estate plain and simple. And the price of online real estate, just like the price of in real life real estate is always going up. CarInsurance.com sold for $49.7 million. Someone sold Insurance.com for $35.6 million. VacationRentals.com went for $35 million. Way back in 2005, LasVegas.com sold for $90 million. The most expensive domain purchase in history so far was Cars.com, which sold for $872 million.

Flipping domains is kind of like flipping real estate. You find an undervalued property that you think will sell for more than what you can buy it for. Then you purchase it, and list it for sale at a higher price on website domain marketplaces. You might not be able to snag any sweet one word domains that sell for millions these days, but there are still a lot of two word and three word gems out there no one's snapped up yet, that you can buy for a few dollars and will sell for hundreds and thousands of dollars to businesses that want them and have the money.

They key to picking out good domains to buy is thinking of ones that are easy to remember, easy to say, short as possible, keyword rich, and end with the dot com extension. Maybe dot net. Dot com is way better. It's like the difference between how many people report vanilla is their favorite flavor of ice cream and how many people report chocolate is. Chocolate is the second most popular ice cream flavor, like dot net is second to dot com, but it's a far distant second to vanilla.

As far as keyword rich goes, you want to look for keywords that are going to be valuable to well capitalized businesses. Do some research into the most valuable niches to blog or advertise in to get an idea of what to look for. But things related to finance, business, real estate, mortgages, law, travel, electronics, cars, retail, health, fitness, beauty, luxury, and fashion are good.

After you buy your domain, what you'll want to list it on domain marketplaces for buyers to find. Flippa is the number one such marketplace. It's one of the top 1000 most visited websites online. It's also a market for buying and selling entire online businesses, websites, and apps. If you go to Flippa's Domains category and click "Editor's Choice," you'll find domains listed anywhere from $10 to $150,000.

MakerMonikers.com is another good place to flip domains. There's no monthly subscription or listing fee, just a percentage commission of your sale as a fee to Maker Monikers. It's only for domains listed between $50 and $500.

GoDaddy, the Internet's number on domain registrar also has a domain marketplace for buyers and sellers. It also has domain auctions eBay style, but for website domains. There is a very small $4.99 per year fee to use it, and a commission fee when your domain sells.

Well, hey this concludes a good list of online side hustles you can definitely get started on.

Remember, don't give up. Be persistent and listen to

that inner-nerd that can help you discover other creative ideas. The internet has made things much easier to learn and also implement.

If you'd like to jump on a call and discuss different strategies to start and scale your online business...let's chat: www.PaulGetter.com/VIP

About the Author

Paul Getter is a friend first and top-tier internet marketer second.Paul's internet marketing career began in desperation. Recently fired and without any prospects, he discovered the power of social media. Without any formal education in marketing, he committed himself to learning every aspect of social media marketing.

Fast forward a few years and he has now spent over one billion dollars running ads and campaigns for his clients, is in the top 1% of ad spenders on Facebook, and has over 1 million followers on Instagram. But Paul knows that platforms like Facebook and Instagram are just tools. They're not the objective. The objective is getting results for his clients. Just a sampling of his successes include boosting the popularity of TV shows, skyrocketing authors onto the New York Times best-sellers list, elevating Fortune 500 companies, and helping numerous A-list celebrities and small-platform personalities gain millions of social media followers. But don't get the wrong idea that Paul only works with household brand names or personalities who have already achieved fame and influence (such as Alex Mehr, Tai Lopez, and Les Brown, just to name just a few). On the contrary, Paul is absolutely passionate about collaborating with anyone who is wholeheartedly dedicated to sharing their awesome ideas with the world.

Paul works with each client in a deeply personal way. People trust him, refer him to their friends and colleagues, and come back to work with him because he cares for them as people. Ethical to the core, Paul has declined numerous lucrative opportunities that didn't align with his principals. He lives in Florida with his wife and three brilliant kids. When not spending time with his family or placing his order a local Starbucks-tall nonfat mocha, please-you might find him in a third-world country camping in huts with no water or electricity. His heart is for the homeless and people in impoverished countries. Paul himself grew up in a low income home, facing many challenges growing up. He has served on the board for a large homeless nonprofit organization that helps those in drug and alcohol rehabilitation. His hobbies include running, reading and optimizing funnels.

Made in the USA
Las Vegas, NV
07 September 2021